THE USBORNE BOOK OF
NURSERY
RHYMES

Illustrated by Radhi Parekh

Designed by Amanda Gulliver

Edited by Caroline Hooper
and Emma Danes

Contents

Little Boy Blue

Little Boy Blue, come blow your horn,

The sheep's in the meadow, the cow's in the corn;

But where is the little boy who looks after the sheep?

He's under a haycock, fast asleep.

Will you go wake him? No, not I,

For if I do, he's sure to cry.

If all the world were paper

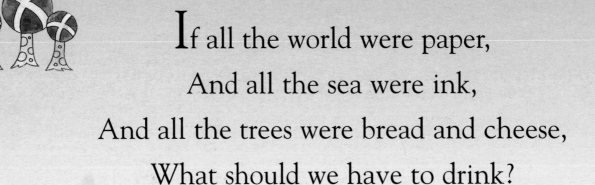

If all the world were paper,
And all the sea were ink,
And all the trees were bread and cheese,
What should we have to drink?

Rub-a-dub-dub

Rub-a-dub-dub,
Three men in a tub,
And who do you think they be?
The butcher, the baker,
The candlestick-maker,
So turn out the knaves, all three.

Jack and Jill

Jack and Jill went up the hill
To fetch a pail of water;
Jack fell down and broke his crown,
And Jill came tumbling after.

Up Jack got, and home did trot,
As fast as he could caper;
He went to bed to mend his head
With vinegar and brown paper.

Goosey, goosey gander

Goosey, goosey gander,
whither would you wander?
Upstairs and downstairs
and in my lady's chamber.

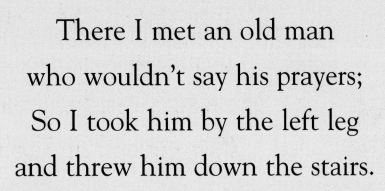

There I met an old man
who wouldn't say his prayers;
So I took him by the left leg
and threw him down the stairs.

Humpty Dumpty

Humpty Dumpty sat on a wall,
Humpty Dumpty had a great fall;
All the King's horses and all the King's men
Couldn't put Humpty together again.

Sing a song of sixpence

Sing a song of sixpence, a pocket full of rye,
Four and twenty blackbirds baked in a pie.
When the pie was opened, the birds began to sing,
Wasn't that a dainty dish to set before the King?

The King was in his counting-house, counting out his money;
The Queen was in the parlour, eating bread and honey;
The maid was in the garden, hanging out the clothes,
When down came a blackbird and pecked off her nose.

Girls and boys, come out to play

Girls and boys, come out to play,
The moon doth shine as bright as day;
Leave your supper and leave your sleep,
And join your playfellows in the street.

Come with a whoop, and come with a call,
Come with a good will or come not at all;
Up the ladder and down the wall,
A penny loaf will serve us all.

Hey diddle, diddle

Hey diddle, diddle,

The cat and the fiddle,

The cow jumped over the moon;

The little dog laughed

To see such fun,

And the dish ran away with the spoon.

Jack Sprat

Jack Sprat could eat no fat,
His wife could eat no lean,
And so between them both, you see,
They licked the platter clean.

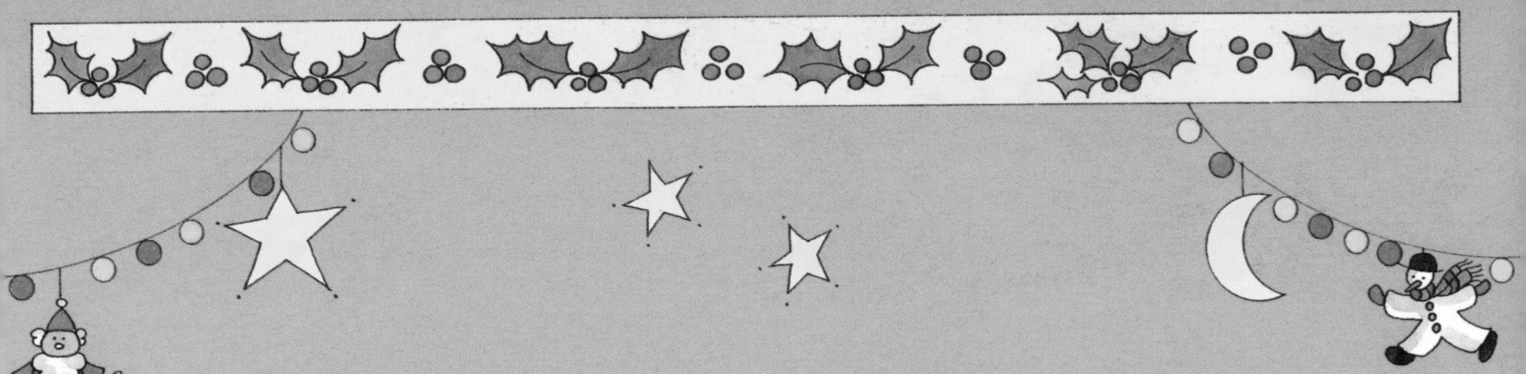

Little Jack Horner

Little Jack Horner
Sat in a corner,
Eating his Christmas pie;
He put in his thumb,
And pulled out a plum,
And said "What a good boy am I!"

Rock-a-bye, baby

Rock-a-bye, baby, on the tree-top,
When the wind blows, the cradle will rock;
When the bough breaks, the cradle will fall,
And down will come baby, cradle and all.

See-saw, Margery Daw

See-saw, Margery Daw,
Johnny shall
have a new
master;

He shall have but a penny a day,
Because he
can't work
any faster.

There was an old woman who lived in a shoe

There was an old woman
Who lived in a shoe,
She had so many children
She didn't know what to do;
She gave them some broth,
Without any bread,
Then whipped them all soundly
And sent them to bed.

There was a crooked man

There was a crooked man,
And he walked a crooked mile,
He found a crooked sixpence
Upon a crooked stile;
He bought a crooked cat,
And it caught a crooked mouse,
And they all lived together
In a little crooked house.

The Owl and the Pussy-cat

The Owl and the Pussy-cat went to sea
In a beautiful pea-green boat,
They took some honey, and plenty of money,
Wrapped up in a five-pound note.
The Owl looked up to the stars above,
And sang to a small guitar,
"O lovely Pussy! O Pussy, my love,
What a beautiful Pussy you are,
You are, you are!
What a beautiful Pussy you are!"

Pussy said to the Owl, "You elegant fowl,
How charmingly sweet you sing!
O let us be married! Too long we have tarried;
But what shall we do for a ring?"
They sailed away, for a year and a day,
To the land where the Bong-tree grows;
And there in a wood a Piggy-wig stood,
With a ring at the end of his nose,
His nose, his nose,
With a ring at the end of his nose.

turn the page

"Dear Pig, are you willing to sell for one shilling
Your ring?" Said the Piggy, "I will."
So they took it away, and were married next day
By the Turkey who lives on the hill.
They dined on mince, and slices of quince,
Which they ate with a runcible spoon;
And hand in hand, on the edge of the sand,
They danced by the light of the moon,
The moon, the moon,
They danced by the light of the moon.

 # Pussy-cat, Pussy-cat

Pussy-cat, Pussy-cat, where have you been?
I've been to London to look at the Queen.
Pussy-cat, Pussy-cat, what did you there?
I frightened a little mouse under a chair.

Simple Simon

Simple Simon met a pieman
  Going to the fair;
Said Simple Simon to the pieman,
  "Let me taste your ware."

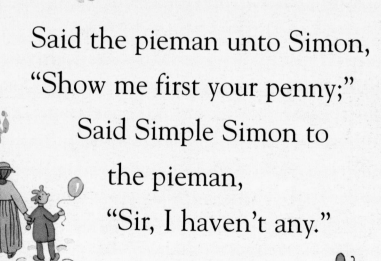

Said the pieman unto Simon,
"Show me first your penny;"
  Said Simple Simon to
    the pieman,
  "Sir, I haven't any."

Ring-a-ring o' roses

Ring-a-ring o' roses,
A pocket full of posies,
A-tishoo! A-tishoo!
We all fall down.

The cows are in the meadow
Eating buttercups,
A-tishoo! A-tishoo!
We all jump up!

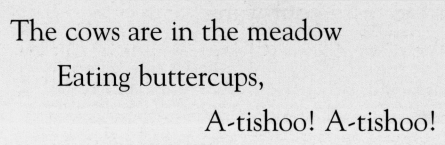

Ride a cock horse

Ride a cock horse to Banbury Cross,
To see a fine lady upon a white horse;
With rings on her fingers
And bells on her toes,
She shall have music wherever she goes.

I had a little nut tree

I had a little nut tree,
Nothing would it bear,
But a silver nutmeg
And a golden pear.

The King of Spain's daughter
Came to visit me,
And all for the sake
Of my little nut tree.

The north wind doth blow

The north wind doth blow,
And we shall have snow,
And what will the robin do then, poor thing?
He'll sit in a barn,
And keep himself warm,
And hide his head under his wing, poor thing!

Lavender's blue

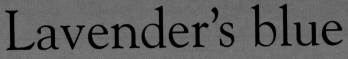

Lavender's blue, dilly, dilly,
Lavender's green,
When I am King, dilly, dilly,
You shall be Queen.

Call up your men, dilly, dilly,
Set them to work,
Some to the plough, dilly, dilly,
Some to the cart.

Some to make hay, dilly, dilly,
Some to make corn,
While you and I, dilly, dilly,
Keep ourselves warm.

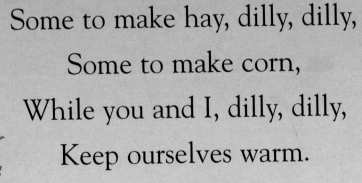

Lavender's green, dilly, dilly,
Lavender's blue,
If you love me, dilly, dilly,
I will love you.

Three blind mice

Three blind mice, three blind mice,
See how they run! See how they run!
They all ran after the farmer's wife
Who cut off their tails with a carving knife;
Did you ever see such a thing in your life
As three blind mice?

Twinkle, twinkle, little star

Twinkle, twinkle, little star,
How I wonder what you are,
Up above the world so high,
Like a diamond in the sky;
Twinkle, twinkle, little star,
How I wonder what you are.

Then the traveller in the dark
Thanks you for your tiny spark.
Could he see which way to go
If you did not twinkle so?
Twinkle, twinkle, little star,
How I wonder what you are.

In the dark blue sky you keep,

And often through my curtains peep;

For you never shut your eye

Till the sun is in the sky.

Twinkle, twinkle, little star,

How I wonder what you are.

Hot cross buns

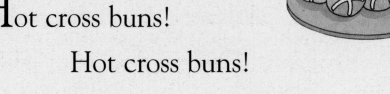Hot cross buns!

Hot cross buns!

One a penny,

Two a penny,

Hot cross buns!

If you have no daughters,

Give them to your sons;

One a penny,

Two a penny,

Hot cross buns!

Pease pudding hot

Pease pudding hot,
Pease pudding cold,
Pease pudding in the pot,
Nine days old.
Some like it hot,
Some like it cold,
Some like it in the pot,
Nine days old.

31

Mary, Mary, quite contrary

Mary, Mary, quite contrary,
How does your garden grow?
With silver bells and cockle shells,
And pretty maids all in a row.

Incy, wincy spider

Incy, wincy spider
Climbed up the spout;
Down came the rain
And washed the spider out.
Out came the sunshine
And dried up all the rain,
So incy, wincy spider
Climbed up the spout again.

One, two, three, four, five

One, two, three, four, five,

Once I caught a fish alive;

Six, seven, eight, nine, ten,

Then I let him go again.

Why did you let him go?

Because he bit my finger so.

Which finger did he bite?

This little finger on the right.

Hickory, dickory, dock

Hickory, dickory, dock!
The mouse ran up the clock;
The clock struck one,
The mouse ran down,
Hickory, dickory, dock!

I'm a little teapot

I'm a little teapot, short and stout,

Here's my handle, here's my spout;

When I see a teacup, hear me shout,

"Lift me up,

and pour me out."

Little Tommy Tucker

Little Tommy Tucker
Sings for his supper.
What shall we give him?
White bread and butter.
How shall he cut it
Without e'er a knife?
How shall he be married
Without e'er a wife?

Pat-a-cake,
pat-a-cake

Pat-a-cake, pat-a-cake, baker's man,
Bake me a cake just as fast as you can;
Pat it and prick it, and mark it with B,
And put it in the oven for baby and me.

Baa, baa, black sheep

Baa, baa, black sheep,
Have you any wool?
Yes, sir, yes sir,
Three bags full:
One for the master,
And one for the dame,
And one for the little boy
Who lives down the lane.

Mary had a little lamb

Mary had a little lamb,
Its fleece was white as snow,
And everywhere that Mary went,
The lamb was sure to go.

It followed her to school one day,
That was against the rule;
It made the children laugh and play,
To see a lamb at school.

And so the teacher turned it out,
But still it lingered near;
And waited for her patiently,
Till Mary did appear.

"Why does the lamb love Mary so?"
The children all did cry;
"Why, Mary loves the lamb, you know,"
The teacher did reply.

Curly Locks

Curly Locks, Curly Locks,

Wilt thou be mine?

Thou shalt not wash dishes

Nor yet feed the swine,

But sit on a cushion

And sew a fine seam,

And feed upon strawberries,

Sugar and cream.

Lucy Locket

Lucy Locket lost her pocket,
Kitty Fisher found it;
Not a penny was there in it,
But a ribbon round it.

Cock-a-doodle-doo

Cock-a-doodle-doo!
My dame has lost her shoe,
My master's lost his fiddling stick,
And doesn't know what to do.

Cock-a-doodle-doo!
My dame has found her shoe,
My master's found his fiddling stick,
So
Cock-a-doodle-doo!

Little Miss Muffet

Little Miss Muffet
Sat on a tuffet,
Eating her curds and whey;
Along came a spider,
Who sat down beside her,
And frightened
      Miss Muffet
          away!

Little Bo-Peep

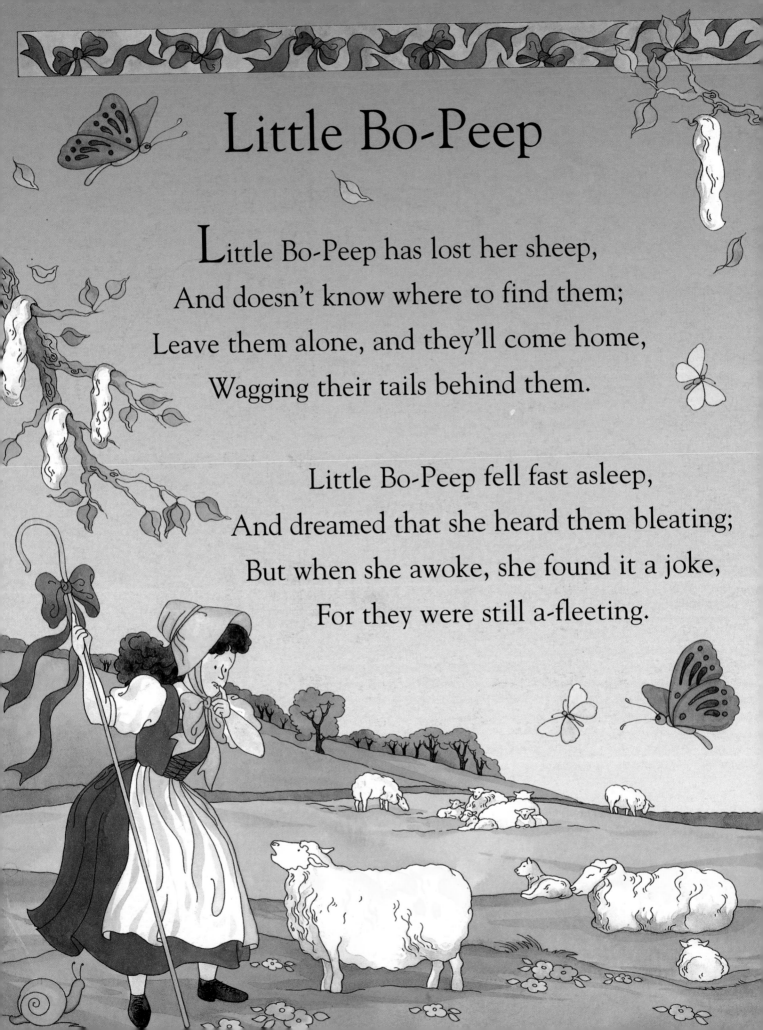

Little Bo-Peep has lost her sheep,
And doesn't know where to find them;
Leave them alone, and they'll come home,
Wagging their tails behind them.

Little Bo-Peep fell fast asleep,
And dreamed that she heard them bleating;
But when she awoke, she found it a joke,
For they were still a-fleeting.

Then up she took her little crook,
Determined for to find them;
She found them indeed, but it made her heart bleed,
For they'd left their tails behind them.

It happened one day, as Bo-Peep did stray
Into a meadow hard by;
That there she espied their tails side by side,
All hung on a tree to dry.

She heaved a sigh, and wiped her eye,
And over the hillocks went rambling,
And tried what she could, as a shepherdess should,
To tack each again to its lambkin.

Games

Some of the nursery rhymes in this book have actions or games that go with them. You can find out about these below.

Hickory, dickory dock

You can use this rhyme to decide who starts a game. As you say the words, point at each player in turn. When the rhyme ends, the person you are pointing at starts the game.

Pat-a-cake, pat-a-cake

Clap your hands while you say the first line, and rub them together in the second line. Next, pretend to prick one of your hands with the first finger of the other. Then, as you say the last line, pretend you are putting a cake into the oven.

Humpty Dumpty

Sit down on the floor with your knees against your chest and wrap your arms around your knees. Rock gently backwards and forwards as you say the rhyme. When you reach the line "Humpty Dumpty had a great fall", roll over backwards. Keep reciting, and without letting go of your knees, try to sit upright again. (This is harder than it sounds!) The player who does this first is the winner.

Pease pudding hot

This rhyme can be used as a clapping game. To play, you have to stand facing a partner. There are four different clapping movements.
1. Clap both hands against your partner's hands.
2. Clap your own hands together.
3. Clap your right hand against your partner's right hand.
4. Clap your left hand against your partner's left hand. Repeat this, saying the lines faster and faster, until one of you makes a mistake.

I'm a little teapot

When you say "Here's my handle", put one hand on your hip. When you say "Here's my spout", put your other arm out to the side like the spout of a teapot. During the last line, lean sideways as if you are pouring the tea.

Ring-a-ring o' roses

While you say this rhyme, all hold hands and step around in a circle. When you say "We all fall down", crouch down as low as you can. Then, as you say "We all jump up", jump up as high as you can.